BEYOND

THE

VEIL

NAVIGATING THE SECRETS OF THE PARANORMAL REALM

TASBEEH AHMAD

For more information, or to book an event, visit :
(tasbeeh-academy.com)

Book design by (Tasbeeh Ahmad)
Cover design by Usama Zaheen (Fashioner Studio)
Quran translation by (https://bridges-foundation.org)

First Edition: May 2023

TASBEEH ACADEMY

CONTENTS

INTRODUCTION

Muslims believe in many paranormal things. In this book, I would like to share our supernatural beliefs as Muslims, why we believe in them, and how we act when we experience something paranormal.

If you accept Islam as your religion, you get all that comes with it, that includes believing in the Quran and all that is within it.

We believe in the paranormal based on what is written in the Holy Quran and the words of Prophet Muhammad; peace be upon him, so even if a Muslim has no experience with paranormal things, he still believes in the Quran and the prophet's words.

The Holy Quran talks about angles, Jinn, envy, magic, Paradise, Hell, and other things that we as Muslims call (Ghayb) (غَيْب) which are things that can only be known by God (Allah).

Note: this is a non-fiction book, and everything written is based on religious beliefs or real experiences.

So, flip the first chapter to know more.

CHAPTER ONE

JINN

If you open the Quran to chapter 72, you will find the entire chapter (Surah) talks about some creatures called (Al-Jinn) (الْجِنْ), which most people refer to as ghosts.

(Jinn) is an Arabic word, and its singular form is (Jinny) (جِنِي), they're creatures that God created from fire, and that's based on verse 15 in chapter 55:

(He created the father of jinn from a smokeless flame of fire)

﴿ وَخَلَقَ ٱلْجَآنَّ مِن مَّارِجٍ مِّن نَّارٍ ﴾

Surah Ar-Rahman, verse 15

And regarding that, fire is not tangible; you can't touch or hold it, but you can feel it, and it can hurt you.

Jinn are powerful, fast, and can travel back and forth between countries in less than a minute. This is evident in chapter 27 of the Quran (Surah An-Naml):

(An Efreet among the Jinn said, "I will bring it to you [prophet Solomon] before you rise from your seat, and indeed, I am certainly strong and trustworthy enough to do it.")

﴿ قَالَ عِفْرِيتٌ مِّنَ ٱلْجِنِّ أَنَا۠ ءَاتِيكَ بِهِۦ قَبْلَ أَن تَقُومَ مِن مَّقَامِكَ وَإِنِّي عَلَيْهِ لَقَوِيٌّ أَمِينٌ ﴾

Surah An-Naml, verse 39

The verse refers to a type of Jinn known as the Efreet (عِفْرِيتٌ) who is more powerful and faster than the other Jinn, who wanted to challenge himself to bring the throne of the Queen in Yemen to Palestine in the kingdom of Prophet Solomon (Solyman) before the prophet could rise from his seat, which means in less than a minute.

***

Chapter 7, verse 27 of the Quran also states that

Jinn are invisible:

(He surely sees you, he and his clan, from

where you cannot see them)

(إِنَّهُ يَرَىٰكُمْ هُوَ وَقَبِيلُهُ مِنْ حَيْثُ لَا تَرَوْنَهُمْ)

Surah Al-A'raf, verse 27

So, they can see you, but you can't see them, but you must be aware that they're around. They are also present when you talk about them; I can sense their presence around me. For instance, someone is tapping my back while I'm writing these words.

***

Jinn are nocturnal creatures and tend to be active from sunset to sunrise, with peak activity at midnight. They also enjoy the beach at night, so it's advised for Muslims to avoid being near the beach during this time.

****

Jinn eat the same food and drink the same beverages as humans do. And that reminds me of when I was 11, and I was alone at home that day. I made a sandwich, left it in the kitchen, and went to my room to get something, but when I returned to the kitchen after a few minutes, the sandwich was gone. My brother-in-law once told me that he was holding a tangerine in his hand, and it fell down as if someone had pushed it; when he looked to catch it, the tangerine had vanished.

****

I also noticed that they speak the same languages as humans; when I was a teenager, I woke up one day and heard two people talking, and when I opened my eyes, I heard someone say:

- Oh, you woke up?

He said it -not only in my native language- but also in my native dialect (the Egyptian dialect).

So, I searched for my family in the apartment, but nobody was there that day. Besides the Quran's teachings, we can say that Jinn are intelligent, just like humans.

***

Another day when I was nine years old, I was sitting alone and not doing anything except daydreaming when suddenly somebody shouted in both my ears simultaneously with a hoarse voice and insulted me. After thinking about it for a while, I concluded that Jinn might try to scare you sometimes to have fun, similar to what we sometimes do by scaring each other as humans.

***

A member of my family told me a story about when he was working in Saudi Arabia, and there was a Jinny who used to tickle him every time he went to sleep. Just imagine someone tickling you, but you can't see him! He said that one day he came back from work, and the Jinny started to tickle him as usual, so he told the Jinny:

- Look, I'm exhausted today, and I need some sleep.

The Jinny stopped and let him sleep.

So, if you ask them to stop doing something and show them that you're not scared of them at all, they might listen to you. This is because they can differentiate between right and wrong and are accountable for their actions like human beings.

There are good and bad Jinn among them, and they themselves acknowledged this in chapter 72 of the Quran:

(And that some of us are righteous, but some of us are less than that: we have been following divergent roads.)

﴿ وَأَنَّا مِنَّا ٱلصَّـٰلِحُونَ وَمِنَّا دُونَ ذَٰلِكَ كُنَّا طَرَآئِقَ قِدَدًا ﴾

Surah Al-Jinn, verse 11

And based on that, they are just like human beings when it comes to religion; there are Muslims, Christians, Jews, and even atheists among them.

***

Jinn live in abandoned places, and because of that, as Muslims, we always seek protection from Allah when entering any abandoned area or house. This reminds me of when I was in high school and had to study hard to get the highest grade possible. So, I needed a quiet place to study. Also, we had another apartment that we used for storage, so I decided to study and sleep there.

Of course, it was not that easy because if a place has been unoccupied for 40 days, Jinn take it as their home and prevent any human from entering or taking it from them. Thanks to Allah, I had my Quran, so I started reading it continuously every day in the apartment and played it on the speaker with a loud sound. Sometimes the Jinn tried to turn the Quran off and play music from my playlist instead. So, I removed all the music from my playlist and left only the Quran.

One night, when I was sleeping in the apartment, I dreamed that my phone was ringing, so I picked up the phone and said:

- who is it?
- he responded: who are you?
- I said: you're the one who called!
- he said: who are you? What are you doing here?
Then I woke up, and I got his message that I was not welcome there, but this is my house, and he can't prevent me from living in my house, even if it hadn't been used for a long time.
I kept focusing on studying and memorizing the Quran, and sometimes they tried to scare me, especially when I recited the Quran; I heard a clap or saw shadows, but I didn't care.

One time, while I was getting my bag to go to school, I caught him staring at me. I didn't see his face because he disappeared in less than a second, but I remember what I saw in that brief moment. He was hairless, and I saw tiny blood vessels beneath his skin. He had large, hooked ears and was shorter than me,

regarding that I'm 150 cm tall

I don't know if I saw his actual appearance or not because I probably didn't see him in his real form.

And by the way, Jinn can take the form of anybody or any animal. and mimic their voices.

One of my friends once told me:

[One day, I delivered an order to one address, and when I rang the bell, I heard the sound of footsteps coming, but the footsteps went back inside again, so I rang the bell for the second time, and the footsteps went towards the door and stopped, but the door didn't open. So, I said:

- Are you going to take the order or not? Then I heard a voice saying: Go away.

So, I realized that it was a Jinny, but I decided to make him open the door, so I kept ringing the bell until he opened it. I saw a skinny man wearing his underwear with messy hair, and his eyes were reddish, like he was on drugs or something. He said with an angry face:

- Didn't I tell you to go away?

- so, I recited:

(I seek refuge in the Lord of mankind and seek his protection)

(QoL aootho be rubby annas)

﴿ قُلْ أَعُوذُ بِرَبِّ ٱلنَّاسِ ﴾

The Holy Quran, Surah An-Nas, verse 1

- As soon as reciting the verse, Jinny shut the door in a second, and I felt hot air blowing in my face, so I went to another apartment and rang the bell. An old woman opened the door, and I asked her about her neighbor, but

- she said: He is a regular guy; why do you ask?

I told her: No, never mind. Can I have the key to the elevator?

She said: yeah! Sure.

So, I looked at the elevator and then at her, but the door was closed. It seems that it was never opened. So I went down to talk with the building guard and asked him about those who live on the ninth floor, but he told me that nobody lives on that floor.]

***

From my friend's story, we can conclude that Jinn can create illusions an make a person see things that do not exist. In chapter 7 of the Quran, verse 116, the Almighty Allah said:

(So, when they cast, they affected the eyes

of the people).

﴾ قَالَ أَلْقُوٓاْ فَلَمَّآ أَلْقَوۡاْ سَحَرُوٓاْ أَعۡيُنَ ٱلنَّاسِ ﴿

Surah Al-A'raf, verse 116

***

Jinn can sometimes communicate with children and make themselves visible to them or scare them. For example, my brother-in- law shared with me that he caught for a moment somebody wearing a jacket and talking to his little nephew, and when he asked his nephew:

- who was that you were talking to?

- he said: he is my imaginary friend.

In another instance, my brother-in-law told me that his other little nephew ran away to his grandma and told her that his stuffed bunny had moved its eyes.

And this can be true because, in general, the prophet Muhammad -peace be upon him- told us that we shouldn't have any living creature's shape, such as pictures or statues, in our homes.

***

Jinn, like humans, can be male or female and engage in marriage. And some people think that Jinn may fall for a particular human, whether he is a male or female. That happens with females specifically, especially females who frequently admire themselves in the mirror or wear revealing clothing. And, of course, if that happened to anyone, this supposed attraction is not a love story but a level that can turn a person's life into a living nightmare.

That's because that person won't be able to get married or have an everyday life like anyone and will hate the idea of marriage, and may suffer from continuous nightmares and sleep paralysis (known as Jathoom or lucid dreams). Those people might also suffer from unexplained scratches or bruises on their bodies and unpleasant odors that emanate from nowhere.

You might be wondering why anyone could harm the person that he loves. And the answer to this, is that there is no love between a Jinny and a human; his only objective is to possess you.

And this reminds me of a story that happened to a relative of mine who was my mom's cousin. She was afflicted with pain and hysteria whenever she heard someone reciting the Quran; in other words, she was possessed.

At that time, she underwent a therapy journey and went to a shaikh (Shaikh is a clergyman in Islam) who specialized in such cases. He began reciting Quran to her until the Jinny inside her spoke through her; the Jinny said that his name was (Anis) and that he loved her, and from what I knew from my mom that her cousin suffered from Anis until she finally healed by the power of the Holy Quran. However, one day she was talking to her sister and said:

- you know what? I missed Anis.

So, he possessed her again to make her suffer, and as a result, Anis made her throw herself from the top of the building.

This tragedy is a stark reminder that no love exists between Jinn and humans; it's just sexual pleasure.

***

The idea that Jinn can possess humans is accurate in specific cases, seeing scratches or bruises on your body for no reason, suffering from sleep paralysis every few days, having nightmares about somebody assaulting you, or raping you, hearing a sound in your mind telling you something like (I love you, you're mine), smelling foul odors coming from nowhere, constantly feeling like somebody is watching you or sleep next to you, all of these are signs that a Jinny is trying to possess you, or may I say **(the consort)** (الْقَرِينْ).

The Qareen

18

CHAPTER TWO

SATANS

The Qareen is a Jinny but with a significant difference: he is hired by the devil himself, whom we call (Iblees, إِبْلِيس).

The Qareen's job is to lead you to make the worst decisions ever in your life, enticing you to corrupt your life with your own hands, and luring you to the path of hell, and whoever does that, whether he was a Jinny or a human, we call him Satan (Shaytan, شَيْطانْ).

Since the beginning of creation, Iblees considered the prophet Adam and all of humankind his enemies.

In chapter 38 of the Quran, Iblees stated to Almighty Allah:

(He said, "Then, by Your Majesty, I will most surely delude them all, except for your sincere chosen servants among them.")

﴿ قَالَ فَبِعِزَّتِكَ لَأُغْوِيَنَّهُمْ أَجْمَعِينَ ﴾

Surah Saad, verse (82)

This was because Allah commanded Iblees to prostrate before Adam, but he refused and disobeyed Allah's divine command and said to the Almighty God:

(He said, "I am better than him; You created me from fire and created him from clay.")

﴿ قَالَ أَنَا خَيْرٌ مِّنْهُ خَلَقْتَنِي مِن نَّارٍ وَخَلَقْتَهُ مِن طِينٍ ﴾

Surah Saad, verse (76)

Therefore, the Almighty Allah cursed Iblees forever, so Iblees formed an army of Jinn to misguide humans.

And this makes me wonder when I see people believing that Jinn can fall in love with a particular human. Basically, Jinn do not see humans only as enemies, but they consider humans as a lower race. So how on earth would someone despise you and love you at the same time?

Even if we suppose that it's possible, he won't consider you more than an enslaved person; he will never see you as a spouse or a partner. He will try to convince you that he loves you, but nobody loves someone to the extent of possessing and torturing him.

Furthermore, every human has a Shaytan or demon who stays with him as his consort or Qareen. The Shaytan has been with you since the first minutes of your life after birth, and he knows everything about you, your personality, your past, your preferences, your weaknesses, and your desire to be loved by someone. So, don't let him use that trap with you.

He is always with you 24 hours a day. However, if you sleep for an extended period, he may get bored and make a noise to wake you up or disturb you with nightmares.

***

The Qareen can also know what you are thinking about. I noticed that when I experienced sleep paralysis (Jathoom) for the first time, I was almost awake but couldn't move and felt a long, tough hand on my back, as if it were made of wood, and I sensed that somebody was hugging me. I didn't know what that was and didn't care either, thinking to myself:
- ok, I can't move anyway, so no problem, go back to sleep.
But suddenly, I felt the hand squeezing me harder, so I said:

(I seek refuge in Allah from the accursed devil)

With a loud voice so, he went away.
- *(Aootho Be-Allah mena shaitan arrajeem)*

أَعُوذُ بِاللَّهِ مِنَ الشَّيطَانِ الرَّجِيمِ

His reaction to my thought seemed like he

could hear what I was thinking, but he did not expect me to say that because from that point on, when Jathoom happens to me, and the

Qareen tries to tie me up, he holds my tongue so that I cannot say the verse. However, I continue to resist until I can say it.

The Almighty Allah tells us in chapter 41 of the Quran:

(And if you are ever spurred by a spurring from Satan, take refuge with Allah; indeed, He is the All-Hearing, the All-Knowing.).

﴿ وَإِمَّا يَنزَغَنَّكَ مِنَ ٱلشَّيْطَٰنِ نَزْغٌ فَٱسْتَعِذْ بِٱللَّهِ إِنَّهُۥ هُوَ ٱلسَّمِيعُ ٱلْعَلِيمُ ﴾

Surah Fussilat, verse (36)

And Speaking of spurring, if you ever find yourself having to choose between two options and you are confused, however, it's clear what is good and what is bad for you; if you find yourself leaning towards the wrong choice and focused on your left ear, you may feel like the Qareen is blowing in your ear, he is delivering thoughts into your mind to make you choose the wrong decision. And if you resist and try to do what is best for you, he will make you feel sleepy. This happens whenever I open the Holy Quran and decide to read it. Your Qareen knows you very well, so he won't tell you: "Don't pray" or "Don't do your work" Instead, he will distract you to prevent you from doing anything beneficial for yourself or others, like what is happening to me right now while I'm writing this book, I enrolled in a course while I was about to engage with my new job as an author, however, taking this course will benefit me, but I know that it's definitely not the right time to take it when I'm focusing on my book. This is exactly what Satan does, distracting you over and over until you find that you haven't completed anything you started or didn't create anything you dreamed of and feel like you're a loser.

***

He also can spur other people to distract you and create fights between you and those who share housing with you for any reason. And while you're fighting, he tries to make both of you say or do stupid things to make you super angry, lose your mind, and make silly decisions. And regarding that, one of the companions of prophet Muhammad, peace be upon him (Solyman ibn Surad) -may Allah be pleased with him- reported:

- (While I was sitting with the Prophet, two men began to insult each other, and the face of one of them turned red, and the veins of his neck got swollen. Prophet Muhammad said: "I know a word that if he said, his rage would go away. If he said, 'I seek refuge with Allah from the accursed devil', his rage would subside.") Sahih/Authentic. - [Al-Bukhari and Muslim].

***

Satans also may hide things like money or keys or anything to create a fight between you and people sharing housing with you, to make you accuse each other of taking personal stuff, which happened once to my aunt, she was coming to our home, and she was late because she couldn't find her key; however, later found them under cover of the bed mattress.

Who would think to hide keys there, and why?

Except for demons who want to start a fight between humans.

And by the way, my aunt doesn't have kids to suspect them of doing that.

My brother-in-law once told a story:
- [I was sleeping beside my baby son, and I opened my eyes and saw a demon in the dark dragging my son slowly.
- I shouted to him: "What are you doing?" He looked at me and seemed surprised that I could see him. He looked scared, with his orange eyes flashing in the dark, because he felt I was not afraid of him.
- I said: *"I seek refuge with Allah from the accursed devil."*
so he disappeared.

When we heard this from my brother-in-law, we thought the demon may have wanted to make my baby nephew fall off the bed and get hurt so that a fight would start between him and his wife.
The prophet Muhammad, peace be upon him, told us:
- (Satan places his throne upon water; then he sends his troops; the nearer to him in

rank are those most skillful in misleading people. One of them comes and says: 'I did this-and-this', to which Satan replies: 'You did nothing.' Then one among them comes and says: 'I did not leave him [the human] until I separated him from his wife.' So, Satan brings him near him and says: 'You did well.)

And you know well what could happen to children when their parents divorce, the children become distracted by their parents' conflict, and the father becomes distant from his kids. When the kids grow up far away from their father, they easily become preys for every satanic friend who can lure them into drugs and crimes. So, you can understand why Satan hates healthy families.

****

I'm not saying that humans have no control over their actions; Of course, we have control and are responsible for our choices.

In the Quran, in chapter 15, the Almighty Allah replied to Satan:

(Indeed, over My servants, you have no authority, except for those who follow you of the deluded ones.)

﴿ إِنَّ عِبَادِي لَيْسَ لَكَ عَلَيْهِمْ سُلْطَـٰنٌ إِلَّا مَنِ ٱتَّبَعَكَ مِنَ ٱلْغَاوِينَ ﴾

Surah Al-Hijr, verse (42)

So, the more you listen to Satan or your Qareen, the more control he will have over you, and by the end, you will find yourself straying from the right path, and your life will become a living hell.

***

For those who have strayed from the right path, the Almighty Allah said in the holy Quran in chapter 58:

(Satan has taken hold of them, and so has caused them to forget the remembrance of Allah.)

﴿ ٱسْتَحْوَذَ عَلَيْهِمُ ٱلشَّيْطَـٰنُ فَأَنسَىٰهُمْ ذِكْرَ ٱللَّهِ ﴾

Surah Al-Mujadalah, verse (19)

The problem is that after luring you to destroy your life, your Qareen will disown you.

In chapter 50 of the Holy Quran:

(His comrade said, "Our Lord, I did not make him exceed all limits, but he was in extreme misguidance.")

﴿ ۞ قَالَ قَرِينُهُۥ رَبَّنَا مَآ أَطْغَيْتُهُۥ وَلَٰكِن كَانَ فِي ضَلَٰلٍ بَعِيدٍ ﴾

Surah Qaf, verse (27)

He is like a lousy friend, trying to make you as bad as he is by tempting you to sin. But when you get in trouble, he will deny responsibility and leave you to face the consequences alone. So far, we have discussed that Qareen is your comrade, and he has a bad influence on you.

But can he possess you?!

CHAPTER THREE

AM, I POSSESSED?

The prophet Muhammad, peace be upon him said:

- (Satan circulates in the son of Adam like blood.) Sahih/Authentic. - [Al-Bukhari and Muslim].

Some scholars have interpreted this statement literally, that Satan can enter the human body and circulates through his veins. Other scholars have viewed it as a metaphor, indicating that Satan is constantly present with the human and never leaves him, just like his blood.

Personally, I lean towards the literal interpretation for a specific reason: physics.

The Almighty Allah said in the Quran (chapter 55):

(He created man [Adam] from clay like [that of] pottery, and He created the Jinn from a smokeless flame of fire).

﴾ خَلَقَ ٱلْإِنسَـٰنَ مِن صَلْصَـٰلٍ كَٱلْفَخَّارِ ﴿
﴾ وَخَلَقَ ٱلْجَآنَّ مِن مَّارِجٍ مِّن نَّارٍ ﴿

Surah Ar-Rahmaan, verse (14, 15).

So regarding that, clay is tangible, moldable, and has a definite size, while flames are intangible and can be expanded or contracted. Therefore, I believe that the Prophet (peace be upon him) meant that Jinn can literally circulate in the human body like blood.

***

It starts when you used to stay alone for a long time, not doing anything but daydreaming or even not thinking at all. For example, this can happen to people who meditate for a long time, sing in the shower, stare at themselves in the mirror for a long time, cry or scream in the bathroom, or deal with boiling water in the bathroom.

In this case, you make yourself an easy target for demons, especially if you are not engaged in anything beneficial. They will try to entice you into sin and may even try to attack you while you sleep. Women, in particular, may experience somebody assaulting them continuously in their dreams, in addition to unexplained pain in their ovaries, which could be a sign that their Qareen is trying to possess them. Of course, it's always a good idea to see a doctor to rule out any physical issues, but if you did, and found nothing wrong with your physical or psychological health, you may start to think that your Qareen is trying to possess you.

A friend of mine once told me that she experienced something invisible that tied her to the bed and raped her multiple times. She tried to resist, but she couldn't do anything. Afterward, she felt pain in her ovaries. So she searched on Google to find out what that might be, and When she started to listen to the Quran, she began to scream, and her father came and took off her headphones. He tried to calm her down by telling her that these kinds of things cannot harm humans, but she told me:

- while my father was speaking, I could not think about anything rather than throttling him.

She continued to read Quran every day and eventually got better.

***

The most dangerous part comes when the victim likes this assault or believes that Jinny really loves him or that Jinny is stronger than him, so the victim stops resisting, and the Qareen may become even more aggressive and possessive. You may have heard about Annalise Michel and the symptoms that she suffered from. These symptoms can develop when no action is taken as soon as the victim feels something is wrong.

You may wonder, what kind of action should be taken in this case? First of all, the victims should check themselves to see if they have any physical or psychological issues, but if there is nothing wrong and they continue to experience Jathoom regularly or smell disgusting odors coming from nowhere, wake up with scratches or bruises on their body for no reason, or start to scream when they hear someone recite the Quran, then the victim should seek treatment from what we as Muslims call

(Ruqia, رُقْيَة).

CHAPTER FOUR

RUQIA

The Ruqia refers to reciting some specific verses and surahs from the Holy Quran as well as some prayers that the prophet Muhammed, peace be upon him, taught us, and it must be recited in Arabic, and as Muslims, we are recommended to recite it every day and night. It acts as a fortress for the one who reads it. You can recite it for yourself or place your hand on the victim's head and recite it. You can also recite the Ruqia while holding your mouth close to pure water and drink the water yourself or give it to someone you suspect that a demon possesses him. and you can use that water to wash yourself or the victim, but not in the bathroom as demons consider it their place.

You start by reciting (chapter 1, Surah Al-Fatihah) in the Holy Quran:

﴿ بِسْمِ ٱللَّهِ ٱلرَّحْمَٰنِ ٱلرَّحِيمِ * ٱلْحَمْدُ لِلَّهِ رَبِّ ٱلْعَٰلَمِينَ * ٱلرَّحْمَٰنِ ٱلرَّحِيمِ * مَٰلِكِ يَوْمِ ٱلدِّينِ * إِيَّاكَ نَعْبُدُ وَإِيَّاكَ نَسْتَعِينُ * ٱهْدِنَا ٱلصِّرَٰطَ ٱلْمُسْتَقِيمَ * صِرَٰطَ ٱلَّذِينَ أَنْعَمْتَ عَلَيْهِمْ غَيْرِ ٱلْمَغْضُوبِ عَلَيْهِمْ وَلَا ٱلضَّآلِّينَ ﴾

(In the name of Allah, the All-Merciful, the Bestower of Mercy, All praise be to Allah, Lord of all realms, the All-Merciful, the Bestower of Mercy, Master of the Day of Recompense. It is You we worship, and it is You we call for help. Guide us to the straight path: the path of those You have blessed, not those who have incurred (Your) wrath, nor those who have gone astray)

***

Then you recite the first five verses of (chapter 2, Surah Al-Baqarah):

﴿ الٓمٓ * ذَٰلِكَ ٱلْكِتَـٰبُ لَا رَيْبَ ۛ فِيهِ ۛ هُدًى لِّلْمُتَّقِينَ * ٱلَّذِينَ يُؤْمِنُونَ بِٱلْغَيْبِ وَيُقِيمُونَ ٱلصَّلَوٰةَ وَمِمَّا رَزَقْنَـٰهُمْ يُنفِقُونَ * وَٱلَّذِينَ يُؤْمِنُونَ بِمَآ أُنزِلَ إِلَيْكَ وَمَآ أُنزِلَ مِن قَبْلِكَ وَبِٱلْأَخِرَةِ هُمْ يُوقِنُونَ * أُو۟لَـٰئِكَ عَلَىٰ هُدًى مِّن رَّبِّهِمْ ۖ وَأُو۟لَـٰئِكَ هُمُ ٱلْمُفْلِحُونَ ﴾

(Alif Lām Mīm. That is the Scripture; there is no doubt about it—a guidance for the mindful (of God), who believe in the (existence of) hidden realms and establish the prayers and spend out of what We have provided them, and those who believe in what has been sent down to you and what has been sent down before you, and regarding the Hereafter they are certain. Those are upon guidance from their Lord, and those are the successful)

***

Then you recite verse (255) of (chapter 2, Surah Al-Baqarah):

﴿ ٱللَّهُ لَآ إِلَٰهَ إِلَّا هُوَ ٱلْحَيُّ ٱلْقَيُّومُ لَا تَأْخُذُهُۥ سِنَةٌ وَلَا نَوْمٌ لَّهُۥ مَا فِي ٱلسَّمَٰوَٰتِ وَمَا فِي ٱلْأَرْضِ مَن ذَا ٱلَّذِي يَشْفَعُ عِندَهُۥٓ إِلَّا بِإِذْنِهِۦ يَعْلَمُ مَا بَيْنَ أَيْدِيهِمْ وَمَا خَلْفَهُمْ وَلَا يُحِيطُونَ بِشَيْءٍ مِّنْ عِلْمِهِۦٓ إِلَّا بِمَا شَآءَ وَسِعَ كُرْسِيُّهُ ٱلسَّمَٰوَٰتِ وَٱلْأَرْضَ وَلَا يَـُٔودُهُۥ حِفْظُهُمَا وَهُوَ ٱلْعَلِيُّ ٱلْعَظِيمُ ﴾

(Allah—there is no god but He, the Living, the All Sustaining. Neither slumber overtakes Him nor sleep. To Him belongs whatever is in the heavens and whatever is in the earth. Who is it who can intercede with Him except by His leave? He knows what is before them and what is behind them, and they do not encompass any of His knowledge except according to what He wills. His kursi has embraced the heavens and the earth, and their preservation does not fatigue Him, for He is the All-High, the Great).

***

Then you recite the last two verses of (chapter 2, Surah Al-Baqarah):

﴿ ءَامَنَ ٱلرَّسُولُ بِمَآ أُنزِلَ إِلَيْهِ مِن رَّبِّهِۦ وَٱلْمُؤْمِنُونَ كُلٌّ ءَامَنَ بِٱللَّهِ وَمَلَـٰٓئِكَتِهِۦ وَكُتُبِهِۦ وَرُسُلِهِۦ لَا نُفَرِّقُ بَيْنَ أَحَدٍ مِّن رُّسُلِهِۦ وَقَالُوا۟ سَمِعْنَا وَأَطَعْنَا غُفْرَانَكَ رَبَّنَا وَإِلَيْكَ ٱلْمَصِيرُ ﴾ ﴿ لَا يُكَلِّفُ ٱللَّهُ نَفْسًا إِلَّا وُسْعَهَا لَهَا مَا كَسَبَتْ وَعَلَيْهَا مَا ٱكْتَسَبَتْ رَبَّنَا لَا تُؤَاخِذْنَآ إِن نَّسِينَآ أَوْ أَخْطَأْنَا رَبَّنَا وَلَا تَحْمِلْ عَلَيْنَآ إِصْرًا كَمَا حَمَلْتَهُۥ عَلَى ٱلَّذِينَ مِن قَبْلِنَا رَبَّنَا وَلَا تُحَمِّلْنَا مَا لَا طَاقَةَ لَنَا بِهِۦ وَٱعْفُ عَنَّا وَٱغْفِرْ لَنَا وَٱرْحَمْنَآ أَنتَ مَوْلَىٰنَا فَٱنصُرْنَا عَلَى ٱلْقَوْمِ ٱلْكَـٰفِرِينَ ﴾

(The Messenger has attained faith in what was sent down to him from his Lord, as have the believers. They have all attained faith in Allah and His angels and His scriptures and His messengers: "We make no distinction between any of His messengers." And they said, "We have heard and obeyed. (Grant us) Your forgiveness, our Lord, for to You is the destiny." Allah does not task any self beyond its capacity. To its credit is what it has earned, and against it is what it has committed. "Our Lord, do not take us to task if we forget or make a mistake. Our Lord, and

do not burden us with a heavy load as You burdened those before us. Our Lord, and do not overburden us with what we have no capability for, and pardon us and forgive us and have mercy upon us. You are our Patron, so support us against the denying people.")

***

Then you recite verses (81,82) of (chapter 17, Surah Al-Esraa):

﴿ وَقُلْ جَاءَ ٱلْحَقُّ وَزَهَقَ ٱلْبَـٰطِلُ إِنَّ ٱلْبَـٰطِلَ كَانَ زَهُوقًا ﴿ وَنُنَزِّلُ مِنَ ٱلْقُرْءَانِ مَا هُوَ شِفَآءٌ وَرَحْمَةٌ لِّلْمُؤْمِنِينَ وَلَا يَزِيدُ ٱلظَّـٰلِمِينَ إِلَّا خَسَارًا ﴾

(And say, "Truth has come while falsehood has withered away; indeed, falsehood is bound to wither away.", And We bestow from on high [send down] of the Recital [Qur'an] that which is a healing and a mercy for the believers, but it does not increase the unjust except in loss)

***

Then you recite verses (97,98) of (chapter 23, Surah Al-Mo'menoon):

﴿ وَقُل رَّبِّ أَعُوذُ بِكَ مِنْ هَمَزَٰتِ ٱلشَّيَٰطِينِ ﴾ ﴿ وَأَعُوذُ بِكَ رَبِّ أَن يَحْضُرُونِ ﴾

(And say, "My Lord, I seek refuge with You from the urgings of the devils, and I seek refuge with You, my Lord, lest they become present with me.")

***

Then you recite the last three chapters of the Quran 3 times:

﴿ قُلْ هُوَ ٱللَّهُ أَحَدٌ * ٱللَّهُ ٱلصَّمَدُ * لَمْ يَلِدْ وَلَمْ يُولَدْ * وَلَمْ يَكُن لَّهُۥ كُفُوًا أَحَدٌ ﴾

(Say, "He is Allah, Uniquely One. Allah, the Indivisible. He begot no one nor was He begotten, and never has there been to Him anyone equivalent.")

(chapter 112, Surah Al-Ekhlas)

***

﴿ قُلْ أَعُوذُ بِرَبِّ ٱلْفَلَقِ * مِن شَرِّ مَا خَلَقَ * وَمِن شَرِّ غَاسِقٍ إِذَا وَقَبَ * وَمِن شَرِّ ٱلنَّفَّاثَتِ فِي ٱلْعُقَدِ * وَمِن شَرِّ حَاسِدٍ إِذَا حَسَدَ ﴾

(Say, "I seek refuge with the Lord of daybreak from the evil of whatever He created, and from the evil of a dusky night when it darkens, and from the evil of sorceresses who blow upon knots, and from the evil of an envier when he envies.")

(chapter 113, Surah Al-Falaq)

***

﴿ قُلْ أَعُوذُ بِرَبِّ ٱلنَّاسِ * مَلِكِ ٱلنَّاسِ * إِلَهِ ٱلنَّاسِ * مِن شَرِّ ٱلْوَسْوَاسِ ٱلْخَنَّاسِ * ٱلَّذِي يُوَسْوِسُ فِي صُدُورِ ٱلنَّاسِ * مِنَ ٱلْجِنَّةِ وَٱلنَّاسِ ﴾

(Say, "I seek refuge with the Lord of mankind, the King of mankind, the God of mankind, from the evil of the sneaky whisperer, who whispers into the chests of

mankind— *(from the whisperers) among the race of unseen being [Jinn] and mankind."*)

(chapter 114, Surah Annas).

***

Then you recite some prayers that the prophet Muhammad, peace be upon him taught us, three times each one:

(بِسْمِ الله أرْقيكَ، مِنْ كُلِّ شَيْءٍ يُؤْذِيكَ، مِنْ شَرِّ كُلِّ نَفْسٍ أَوْ عَيْنِ حَاسِدٍ، اللهُ يَشْفِيكَ، بِسمِ اللهِ أُرقيكَ)

(In the name of Allah, I recite over you, (to protect you) from everything that harms you, from the evil of every soul or envious eye, Allah will cure you, in the name of Allah I recite over you)

***

(أَعُوذُ بِكَلِمَاتِ اللهِ التَّامَّةِ مِنْ شَرِّ مَا خَلَقَ)

(I seek refuge in the Perfect Words of Allah from the evil of what He has created.)

***

(أعوذُ بِكلماتِ اللَّهِ التَّامَّةِ ، مِن كلِّ شيطانٍ وَهامَّةٍ ومن كلِّ عينٍ لامَّةٍ)

(With Allah's perfect words, I seek Allah's protection from every devil, poisonous creature, and evil eye.)

***

(أَعُوذُ بِكَلِمَاتِ اللهِ التَّامَّةِ مِنْ شَرِّ مَا خَلَقَ، وَذَرَأَ، وَبَرَأَ، وَمِنْ شَرِّ مَا يَنْزِلُ مِنَ السَّمَاءِ، وَمِنْ شَرِّ مَا يَعْرُجُ فِيهَا، وَمِنْ شَرِّ فِتَنِ اللَّيْلِ وَالنَّهَارِ، وَمِنْ شَرِّ كُلِّ طَارِقٍ إِلَّا طَارِقًا يَطْرُقُ بِخَيْرٍ، يَا رَحْمَنُ)

(I seek refuge in the Perfect Words of Allah - which neither the upright nor the corrupt may overcome - from the evil of what He created, of what He made, from the evil of what descends from the heavens, and of what rises to them, from the evil of what He created in the earth, and of what emerges from it, from the evil trials of night and day, and from the

evil of every night visitor, except the night visitor who comes with good. O Merciful Allah)

***

(بِسْمِ اللَّهِ الَّذِي لَا يَضُرُّ مَعَ اسْمِهِ شَيْءٌ فِي الْأَرْضِ وَلَا فِي السَّمَاءِ وَهُوَ السَّمِيعُ الْعَلِيمُ)

(In the Name of Allah, Who with His Name nothing can cause harm in the earth nor the heavens, and He is the All-Hearing, the All- Knowing.)

***

Then you recite this prayer 7 times:

(أَعُوذُ بِاللَّهِ وَقُدْرَتِهِ مِنْ شَرِّ مَا أَجِدُ وَأُحَاذِرُ)

(I seek refuge in Allah's might and power from the evil of what I am experiencing and trying to avert.)

***

Then you recite this prayer once:

(اللَّهُمَّ إِنِّي أَسْأَلُكَ الْعَافِيَةَ فِي الدُّنْيَا وَالآخِرَةِ، اللَّهُمَّ إِنِّي أَسْأَلُكَ الْعَفْوَ وَالْعَافِيَةَ فِي دِينِي وَدُنْيَايَ وَأَهْلِي وَمَالِي، اللَّهُمَّ استُرْ عَوْرَاتِي، وآمِنْ رَوْعَاتِي، اللَّهُمَّ احْفَظْنِي مِنْ بَيْنِ يَدَيَّ، ومِنْ خَلْفِي، وَعن يَمِينِي، وعن شِمالِي، ومِن فَوْقِي، وأعُوذُ بِعَظَمَتِكَ أنْ أُغْتَالَ مِنْ تَحتِي)

(O Allah, I ask you for well-being in this world and the Next. O Allah, I ask you for forgiveness and well-being in my faith, this world, my family, and my property. O Allah, veil my faults and calm my fears. O Allah, give me protection before me, behind me, on my right, left, and above me. And I seek refuge by Your might from being overwhelmed from under me.)

***

During the Ruqia, the victim may scream or cry, which is a sign that the demon inside the victim is being tortured by the Ruqia.

After the Ruqia, the victims may feel extreme pain in their body or bones, which is a sign that the Ruqia is effective, and this pain will release day by day if you continue to recite the Ruqia every day.

If you recited the Ruqia in pure water and drink it, you may feel like vomiting; If you are possessed, after vomiting, you will feel better.
But, if you don't feel anything strange, then there is nothing wrong with you, and you are completely fine.

You may wonder why you should repeat the verse 3 or 7 times. Well, from my experience, repeating the verse or the prayer has a greater significance in curing the victim, especially if you recite every verse and focus on its meaning, not just reciting while thinking of something else.

***

some people make a common mistake during the Ruqia, that if the demon speaks through the victim's voice, they start talking to the demon, and this is very dangerous, especially for the one trying to cure the victim because the demons or satans are very sly creatures; they will convince you to cooperate with them first, but afterward, you will find yourself under their control.

***

Also, you must recite the Ruqia every day for at least a month to get the best results. Reciting Chapter 2 or surah Al-Baqarah also helps. And if you sustained on reciting surah Al-Baqarah every day; it will cleanse your body and your house from any demonic creature, and guarantee that your home will not be haunted.

The prophet Muhammad -peace be upon him – said that reading Surah Al-Baqarah daily is a Blessing and leaving it is grief and the sorcerers cannot beat the one who reads it.

But note that there are some cases in the Ruqia that may not cure the victim: for instance, if the victim likes the demon or thinks that the demon loves him, or feels special because he is possessed and the demons will deliver all of these thoughts to the victim to make him stop reciting or listening to the Ruqia and have no motivation to be cured.

Some people who don't know what should be recited in the Ruqia, seek help from any shaikh or any specialist scholar. However, if you see that shaikh repeating phrases in a weird language or asking you to slaughter an animal or drink blood or buy herbs and burn them or do anything other than the Ruqia, then you must know that this is not a shaikh but a

Magician.

CHAPTER FIVE

MAGIC

I'm sorry to tell you that magic, witchcraft, wizardry, or sorcery are not as cool or entertaining as portrayed in movies. It is a hazardous practice based on cooperating with demons or Satan to obtain what you desire, and you know the cost of that.

Exactly, it's selling your soul to them. Essentially, it is like signing a contract with them, except that: they can break it anytime. You might wonder what the issue is if demons can make you wealthy or fulfill your wishes. So, let me tell you what happened to a wizard who practiced magic or sorcery for over 25 years.

The x wizard said:

- [I inherited sorcery from my father. When I
was a baby, about six months old, I started
seeing demons and having epileptic seizures
because of it. So, when my mother told my
father about this, he agreed to sell my soul to
the demons, and the epileptic seizures
stopped.

When I turned 14, my father passed away;
I used to walk in the woods near my
village, and there I began to see beautiful
girls walking around, but they weren't
girls. They were female demons.

Once when I went out far away from my
village, I found a donkey tied up to a tree
next

to a house. I thought someone left the donkey there, so I rode it to take me home because my home was so far away. So I rode the donkey until I reached a rugged place, and the donkey refused to go further. I hit it twice on its neck, but it didn't move, so I was about to hit it the third time, but the donkey turned its face towards me and said:

- "Do you think I'm a donkey? So, you can hit me?!"

and it spoke with a woman's voice.

I was 15 at the time, and honestly, I got scared and tried to hit it the third time, but it disappeared, and I lost consciousness.

Some people in my village found me and brought me to my mom. I told her what happened; so she tied me up and asked a group of men in my town to take me to a sheikh because she thought I was possessed. When I saw the sheikh, I knew he was not a real sheikh but a magician. He had one demon beside him, and I had seven, the magician said: - "Let him go. He has his father's dignity."

so my mom had no choice but to chain me to my bed because she was afraid I would follow in my father's track.

I was chained for three years, but my mother didn't know that the demons had unchained me at night and let me out of the house.

Later, I started to feel the desire to eat children. I resisted this urge so hard, but if I had the chance to get a child, he would never survive. Thank God I never acted on that impulse.

I found out later that my father used to eat children and adults, and if he had a chance to kidnap any human, he would eat them.

The demons taught me about magic and sorcery, and they promised me that I would become rich, so I took it seriously and practiced witchcraft and sorcery for 25 years. But the demons were so sly that they didn't let me have any cash in my hand, so I wouldn't stop practicing magic. So whenever one gave me money, the demons convinced me to spend it here and there so that I would need to sell my magic services again and again and never stop.

The point is that demons won't benefit you in any way; if they do, they take something more valuable from you. So even If I delayed any demand from them, they were harming me too much.
I was like an enslaved to them.

Once while I was practicing magic, I felt a sudden urge to sleep, and I dreamed that I had died in my hometown. I saw myself calling for help, but no one could hear me. Then, I found myself in my grave, and I saw a group of people coming and told me:
-"Go perform ablution and pray."
I said: where?!
So they pointed somewhere, where I looked and saw boiling water. I tried to run away, but a copper hand appeared from the ground, grabbed my leg, and threw me into the boiling water.

I woke up, and I was screaming because of that nightmare, and I asked myself:
-"What did I do that made the demons so angry with me?"
And I decided to go pray to God for the first time.

As soon as I decided, I felt like my body was boneless and could barely move. I tried so hard until I reached the washroom and made an ablution. When I started to pray, a bunch of demons surrounded me and wanted to prevent me, and every time I tried to close my eyes to avoid seeing them, I felt like nails were piercing through my eyes.

I could hardly complete the prayer, and after a while, I went to the mosque to pray the Dawn prayer. However, when I opened the Quran in the mosque, I found that the letters were separated and felt that I had earned God's Anger to the point that I couldn't even read the Holy Quran, so I decided to repent from all of my heart.

After I returned, the demons threatened me that they would kill my family if I repented from practicing magic. I insisted on repenting, so after a while, I found my wife's belly was flat; she was in the ninth month of pregnancy. The demons told me they killed the baby inside her and would kill my other two sons if I insisted on repenting.

After that, I told my wife everything and asked her:

- "Would you like me to repent from practicing magic and lose our kids or not repent, and everything will stay the same?" Her response surprised me; she told me:

- "Even if we are going to lose our children now, we will meet them in paradise, but if you don't repent, we are all going to be in hell forever, so don't hesitate to repent to God because practicing magic is a huge sin and we can't afford the punishment of hell."

She held those words in her heart for a long time and was never pleased that I practiced magic.

Later, the demons threatened me again when they saw that I still insisted on repenting. But my response was one:

- "I'll never practice magic again."

After one moment, I saw my 9-year-old son swell until his eyes fell out of his face, and he fell dead. Then, the demons shouted at me:

- "If you don't take back your decision, we will kill your other son."

But I refused, so after 20 minutes, my little son died the same way.

I lost consciousness, and my mental state was unstable for three months. After that, the demons continued threatening me that they would kill my wife if I insisted on repenting. But after all that loss, I decided not to return to magic.

A few hours later, I found my wife bleeding profusely, so I took her to the hospital.

The doctors put her on every medical device possible and checked her thoroughly, but all the records and reports showed that she was perfectly fine. However, she was bleeding at that time, and the doctors didn't know what to do, and she died in front of my eyes, and nothing saved me after that except the Holy Quran and prayers.].

***

After this x magician's story, you may wonder why practicing magic is considered a major sin in Islam. The reason is that magic is based on causing harm and inflicting pain on others, as the Almighty Allah told us in the Quran:

(And they followed what the devils read during the reign of Solomon. But never did Solomon deny [Blaspheme]; rather, it was the Satans who denied, teaching people sorcery and what was sent down in Babylon to the two angels Harut and Marut. And they do not teach anybody until they say, "We are but a means of trial, so do not deny (faith)." Even so, they learn from them the means to cause separation between a man and his spouse—

but never could they harm anyone except by Allah's leave. And they learn what would harm them and not benefit them. Yet they did know that whoever purchased it [magic, witchcraft] would have no share in the Hereafter. So indeed, how miserable is what they sold themselves for, if they only knew!)

﴿ وَٱتَّبَعُواْ مَا تَتْلُواْ ٱلشَّيَـٰطِينُ عَلَىٰ مُلْكِ سُلَيْمَـٰنَ وَمَا كَفَرَ سُلَيْمَـٰنُ وَلَـٰكِنَّ ٱلشَّيَـٰطِينَ كَفَرُواْ يُعَلِّمُونَ ٱلنَّاسَ ٱلسِّحْرَ وَمَآ أُنزِلَ عَلَى ٱلْمَلَكَيْنِ بِبَابِلَ هَـٰرُوتَ وَمَـٰرُوتَ وَمَا يُعَلِّمَانِ مِنْ أَحَدٍ حَتَّىٰ يَقُولَآ إِنَّمَا نَحْنُ فِتْنَةٌ فَلَا تَكْفُرْ فَيَتَعَلَّمُونَ مِنْهُمَا مَا يُفَرِّقُونَ بِهِۦ بَيْنَ ٱلْمَرْءِ وَزَوْجِهِۦ وَمَا هُم بِضَآرِّينَ بِهِۦ مِنْ أَحَدٍ إِلَّا بِإِذْنِ ٱللَّهِ وَيَتَعَلَّمُونَ مَا يَضُرُّهُمْ وَلَا يَنفَعُهُمْ وَلَقَدْ عَلِمُواْ لَمَنِ ٱشْتَرَىٰهُ مَا لَهُۥ فِي ٱلْأَخِرَةِ مِنْ خَلَـٰقٍ وَلَبِئْسَ مَا شَرَوْاْ بِهِۦٓ أَنفُسَهُمْ لَوْ كَانُواْ يَعْلَمُونَ ﴾

Chapter 2, verse 102, Surah Al-Baqarah

***

This reminds me of a girl I met in high school. The first time I saw her, her friends surrounded her. I looked at her, and she was unable to control her tongue or speak; her saliva wet her blouse because she couldn't swallow it.

I thought she might be suffering from an illness, and because I didn't know her, I just prayed that Allah would heal her.

A year later, I met that girl again in school. She looked healthy, so I asked her what had happened. She told me that a magician or witch had practiced magic on her, and she had suffered from multiple illnesses. She told me that demons sometimes held her tongue and didn't let her speak or swallow her saliva or held her colon so that she couldn't go to the toilet for a month or more. The demons also made her hate her family, friends, and anyone who tried to help her.

Thank God she had been healed by reciting the Quran and Ruqia, and now she is okay.

I didn't ask her who did that to her because in most cases, the one who did it is someone close to her and has access to her stuff.

***

In rural regions, some magicians take advantage of people by convincing them that there is a treasure in their village, and to find it, they must sacrifice their children as an oblation for demons, but later, the magician will ask the family for much money for any stupid reason. When the magician runs away with the money, the family finds out that they are under a scam and that there is no treasure. Unfortunately, they killed their children for nothing and are all going to jail, and this scam has happened to many people in rural areas.

***

In my home country [Egypt], a whole village was burned down because of sorcery and magic. The people there said that every house was catching fire from nowhere and for no reason. And many people died there because of that.

***

You can understand why people used to burn witches in the past, and of course, I don't condone it because, in Islam, it is entirely forbidden to burn any living creature and torture him that way. However, according to

Islamic laws, magicians should be executed if caught practicing sorcery with solid proof unless they repented before they were caught. Some scholars said that they should only be executed if somebody died because of their sorcery.

Nowadays, witches have stores and sell their books in public, thanks to the media, and the problem with this is that even reading or hearing a sorcery spell can cause a crisis for whoever reads or hears it.

***

Sometimes, the magic is written and buried in an abandoned place or the victim's house. Therefore, you must find it and destroy it. Perhaps you can recite the Ruqia on the water and put those magical items into the water that has the Ruqia. Also, some verses in the Quran have the power to invalidate magic, and you can add them to the Ruqia, especially when you repeat them three times in the Ruqia every day and night. These verses include:

From verses (117 to 122) in Surah Al-A'raf :

﴿ ۞ وَأَوْحَيْنَا إِلَى مُوسَى أَنْ أَلْقِ عَصَاكَ فَإِذَا هِيَ تَلْقَفُ مَا يَأْفِكُونَ * فَوَقَعَ ٱلْحَقُّ وَبَطَلَ مَا كَانُواْ يَعْمَلُونَ * فَغُلِبُواْ هُنَالِكَ وَٱنقَلَبُواْ صَٰغِرِينَ * وَأُلْقِيَ ٱلسَّحَرَةُ سَٰجِدِينَ * قَالُوٓاْ ءَامَنَّا بِرَبِّ ٱلْعَٰلَمِينَ * رَبِّ مُوسَى وَهَٰرُونَ ﴾

(And We revealed to Moses: "Throw your staff," and, lo and behold, it swallowed what they were faking! Thus the truth came to pass, and what they were doing went to waste. So there and then they were overcome, and they returned, utterly belittled. Then the sorcerers fell prostrating. They said, "We have attained faith in the Lord of all realms, the Lord of Moses and Aaron.")

Chapter 7 in the Quran.

***

From verses (81 to 82) in Surah Yunus, chapter 10:

﴿ فَلَمَّآ أَلْقَوْاْ قَالَ مُوسَىٰ مَا جِئْتُم بِهِ ٱلسِّحْرُّ إِنَّ ٱللَّهَ سَيُبْطِلُهُۥ إِنَّ ٱللَّهَ لَا يُصْلِحُ عَمَلَ ٱلْمُفْسِدِينَ * وَيُحِقُّ ٱللَّهُ ٱلْحَقَّ بِكَلِمَٰتِهِۦ وَلَوْ كَرِهَ ٱلْمُجْرِمُونَ ﴾

(So, when they threw, Moses said, "What you produced is sorcery; indeed, Allah will nullify it; indeed, Allah does not set aright the work of the corrupters. And Allah upholds the truth with His words, even if the criminals dislike it.")

*****

And verse 69 from chapter 20, Surah Taha:

﴿ وَأَلْقِ مَا فِي يَمِينِكَ تَلْقَفْ مَا صَنَعُوٓاْ إِنَّمَا صَنَعُواْ كَيْدُ سَٰحِرٍّ وَلَا يُفْلِحُ ٱلسَّاحِرُ حَيْثُ أَتَىٰ ﴾

(And cast what is in your right hand—it will swallow what they have crafted; what they have crafted is only a sorcerer's trickery, for the sorcerer will not succeed wherever he may go.".)

***

But don't worry if you didn't find those magic items, Reciting the Ruqia every day should be enough to invalidate any magic or sorcery. Some sorcerers recite their spells on water, so be careful before stepping on any water you don't know its source.

You might wonder how to identify a magician since they often hide behind the facade of religious men or women, psychics, or any other acceptable persona in society. And can you ask them for a favor without hurting anyone?

If you think like that, you'll be the first one to get hurt because basically, If the magician summons demons to you, you'll live your life in fear.

This happened to many people who accidentally read or heard a sorcery spell by mistake, so imagine what would happen if you went to a magician with your own will.

The Almighty Allah mentioned in the Quran in chapter 72, Surah Al-Jin:

﴿ وَأَنَّهُ كَانَ رِجَالٌ مِّنَ ٱلْإِنسِ يَعُوذُونَ بِرِجَالٍ مِّنَ ٱلْجِنِّ فَزَادُوهُمْ رَهَقًا ﴾

(And that certain men among humans used to seek refuge in certain men among the Jinn, but they only increased them in confusion.)

Moreover, the demons will know everything about you through your Qareen, who is also a demon. Therefore, if the magician knows you are wealthy, for example, he will ask you for much money, and he can't guarantee the result. In addition, the x magicians said:

- Demons won't benefit anyone from human beings because they see us as enemies; the devil ordered them to lead all children of Adam to the path of hell. Therefore, don't believe anyone who claims to contact spirits and claims that they are kind because demons are cunning creatures who will convince you that they are on your side until you fall into their trap and become their puppet.

And that brings us to some magicians who claim that they can predict the future like

Psychics.

CHAPTER SIX

PSYCHICS

Magicians sometimes hide behind the masks of fortune tellers or psychics if that sort of persona is acceptable in the society around them.

The difference between sorcerers, witches, and psychic magicians is that psychics may not cause as much harm as sorcerers cause to people. This is because what psychics and sorcerers have in common is that they both cooperate with demons and Jinn to obtain hidden information about people through their comrades (Qareens) or to know their future.

But before jumping to any conclusions, you must know that future destiny is a sort of (Ghayb, غَيْب) which is something that can only be known from God. So, how can Jinn know about the future?

The Almighty Allah mentioned in chapter 72, Surah Al-Jinn, that the Jinn said:

(And that we sought to reach the heaven and found it filled with stern guards and meteors. And that we used to take up positions to listen in, but whoever listens now finds a meteor in wait for him. And that we do not know whether ill has been desired for those on earth, or if their Lord has desired prudence for them.)

﴿ وَأَنَّا لَمَسْنَا ٱلسَّمَآءَ فَوَجَدْنَٰهَا مُلِئَتْ حَرَسًا شَدِيدًا وَشُهُبًا * وَأَنَّا كُنَّا نَقْعُدُ مِنْهَا مَقَٰعِدَ لِلسَّمْعِ فَمَن يَسْتَمِعِ ٱلْأَنَ يَجِدْ لَهُۥ شِهَابًا رَّصَدًا ﴾

Surah Al-Jinn, verses (8 to 10)

The verses indicate that Jinn used to ascend to the heavens and eavesdrop on the angels' discussing matters related to the future of people on Earth, and some scholars suggest that they used their large numbers to climb on top of each other to reach the sky. And other scholars said that some of them can fly. But anyone of Jinn who attempts this now will be met with a meteor that will burn them.

The Jinn used to know the future through this method. But basically, it doesn't mean that Jinn is no longer trying to eavesdrop on the angels in the heavens.

They still try to do so. The Almighty Allah mentioned in chapter 37, Surah As-Saaffat:

(Indeed, We have adorned the lowest heaven with an adornment, the planets, and as a protection against every defiant devil. They cannot eavesdrop on the Higher Assembly, for they get bombarded from every side— repelled, and they will have an unremitting punishment, except for one who snatched a fragment and was then pursued by a piercing meteor.)

﴿ إِنَّا زَيَّنَّا ٱلسَّمَآءَ ٱلدُّنْيَا بِزِينَةٍ ٱلْكَوَاكِبِ * وَحِفْظًا مِّن كُلِّ شَيْطَٰنٍ مَّارِدٍ * لَّا يَسَّمَّعُونَ إِلَى ٱلْمَلَإِ ٱلْأَعْلَىٰ وَيُقْذَفُونَ مِن كُلِّ جَانِبٍ * دُحُورًا وَلَهُمْ عَذَابٌ وَاصِبٌ * إِلَّا مَنْ خَطِفَ ٱلْخَطْفَةَ فَأَتْبَعَهُ شِهَابٌ ثَاقِبٌ ﴾

Surah A-Saffat, verses (6 to 10)

Just as a note, when Allah refers to Himself in the verse as (We), it is to glorify Himself as plural pronouns can refer to glory in the Arabic language. It does not refer to multiple Gods; there is only One God.

The verses explain that Jinn can no longer eavesdrop on the angels' conversations, except for the rare instance where they may catch a word or two. If they do so, a piercing meteor chases them and burns them. Muslim scholars clarified that the meteor burns them but does not kill them. If Allah Hadn't excluded the possibility that a demon may snatch a word or two, we could have said that Jinn cannot hear anything.

In conclusion, Jinn can hear only a word or two from the angels' conversation, and then they may convey it to a psychic before the meteor burns them. The psychic then fabricates a story, and this story may coincidentally occur, and this brings us to the Arabic quote:

"The fortune tellers always lie even if they said facts."

This quote highlights that even if the fortune-teller's story is true, they still lie because they do not know the future. And, of course, the Almighty Allah Is the One Who Allows the demons to take that fragment due to His Great Wisdom, Which we may not understand. And He Can Take that ability from the demons if He Wants.

It's also important to remember that Jinn would not willingly put themselves in danger of being burned for free. If they reveal information to a psychic, they will likely ask for a significant sacrifice in return. Therefore, one should be cautious before visiting a psychic or fortune teller and potentially becoming the reason for sacrificing a child.

However, this does not mean that all psychics and fortune tellers engage in such activities. Some individuals may accidentally involve themselves in psychic activities without intending to.

And that reminds me of a story about a 17-year-old girl named Dina who called an Egyptian TV show and said that she suffers from an illness that causes her to cry blood instead of tears. She hoped that people would donate to her through the TV show so she could be cured of her illness.

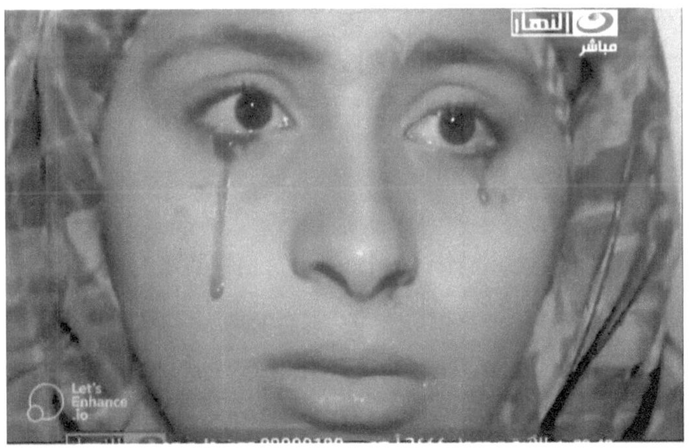

Dina said that her life was normal until about a year ago when she began experiencing vertigo and poor vision in her left eye. After that, her eye started to bleed, and her condition worsened to the point that blood would cover her entire face due to bleeding from her eyes. Her father took her to the doctor, who requested a quick brain x-ray, the x-rays showed that her brain was completely normal, and she was supposed to be okay, according to medical reports.

But her condition continued to worsen to the point that when she closed one eye, the other eye began to bleed, and when she closed both of her eyes, her nose and mouth started to bleed. Even when she covers her nose and mouth with cotton, her nails start to bleed.

The doctor attempted to administer medication through a cannula, but he noticed the drugs were excreted through her eyes and mouth. This led the doctor to doubt that there might be an underlying cause for these symptoms. So he asked Dina if anything unusual was happening to her or if she had been having creepy nightmares.

Dina said that she always had a nightmare of someone chasing and trying to assault her, and that nightmare began after she fell in the toilet once. Since then, her life has become a living nightmare.

The doctor decided to keep Dina in the hospital while the doctors performed a thorough medical analysis on her and waited for the resulting reports.

During her stay, a patient who shared the room with Dina mentioned that she heard Dina talking to herself in her sleep and suggested that the Ruqia should be recited on her. Dina's sister then contacted a Sheikh named Muhammad to perform the Ruqia on her.

When Sheikh Muhammad arrived at the hospital, Dina said that she could hear a very loud sound of footsteps coming from a distance, and even when he stopped walking, she said she couldn't hear anything until he entered the room.

Shaikh Muhammad started to talk to Dina for a while, then he began reciting the Ruqia, and Dina immediately began bleeding, writhing in pain, and eventually, she lost consciousness. When she regained consciousness, her family told her that her voice had changed and sounded like a man's voice.

At this point, Dina's family realized they were dealing with something beyond medical or scientific explanations. And because there was no medical reason to keep Dina for that long in the hospital, the doctors released her.

Shaikh Muhammad started to recite the Ruqia to Dina in sessions.

During these sessions, Dina felt like someone was squeezing her throat, and one time Dina's sister was talking to her, suddenly when Dina heard her sister calling her name, Dina said:

- "I'm not Dina; I'm Mari."

Shaikh Muhammad told Dina that if anything happened to him, it would be because of the demons possessing her.

Unfortunately, he died three days later. Her family tried to reassure her that his death was not because of her. And typically, that is true because we believe as Muslims that every soul has a precise moment of death that will never delay or come early.

Dina's family called another shaikh to continue the Ruqia sessions, but he disappeared for two months. When they finally spoke to him again, he said that he had come to their home multiple times, but they were unable to see or hear him.

Since then, they have been reaching out to every shaikh they can find, but most only come for two sessions before stopping or not being able to come due to unforeseen circumstances.

But all the Shaikhs agreed that Dina is possessed by a clan of 1000 demons, not just one or two.
Dina said that after that, she started seeing humanoid bodies with animals' heads, and

while telling her story on the TV show, she said:
- "Is there anyone reciting Quran here? If someone is reciting Quran now, please stop." It was a famous Shaikh named Amr Alleithy who was reciting the Quran during Dina's episode, and he was supposed to have a promo session after her in that TV show.

He sat with Dina and told her that the Jinn are weak against the Quran and that she shouldn't be afraid of them. And while he was speaking, Dina looked at him as if she wanted to kill him, and as soon as he started reciting the Ruqia, she became enraged, and her eyes began to bleed in front of the camera. So the Shaikh called out to her:
- "Dina, can you hear me?"
Then she lost consciousness, and the whole camera crew felt a presence behind them.

After Dina regained consciousness, she said she felt like vomiting and had an extreme headache. The Shaikh explained that the headache is a symptom of a type of Jinn that targets people who engage in fortune-telling or psychic activities. At this point, Dina admitted to practicing fortune-telling since childhood, and everything she predicted had come true. She believed it was a gift from Allah that she was talented in fortune-telling. But the Shaikh explained that it is a huge sin that drives angels away and urged her to repent.

Dina repented and continued the Ruqia sessions with Shaikh Amr. Two weeks later, when the TV show contacted her again, she said that her eyes had stopped bleeding, and she was feeling better.

***

Honestly, that episode was subject to falsification from a large group of viewers, but the TV show representative said that it's impossible for a 17-year-old girl to sacrifice her reputation and entire career to fabricate a story on a TV show. This means that she was really suffering. Additionally, if what was coming out of her eyes was anything other than real blood, it should have left a stain on her face, meaning it was real blood. And they can testify that they were just listening to her story, but suddenly she cried blood in front of them all and they never expected that.

And who knows, maybe that episode was a message from God that even these kinds of cases can be cured.

But think about this: just because she used to practice fortune-telling through some games when she was a kid, a whole clan of Jinn possessed her.

However, it's unnecessary to be possessed because of practicing fortune telling as a game because demons and Jinn are sly creatures that will whisper to you to practice it as a game first and help you for free to convince you that you're talented with psychical activities. So, you will try to improve your claimed talent, and during that, you will find yourself reciting sorcery spells, and by the end, you will find yourself trapped in this craft. Just like drug dealers, they give you the first doses for free until you become an addict.

You may think that if there are religious Jinn, they may help you as Jinn who believe in God and won't hurt you. However, that's not true because religious Jinn are committed to the treaty that they won't serve any human after Prophet Solomon.

Some people may claim that ghosts or Jinn rescued them from dangerous situations before, but let me tell you that the invisible creatures that saved you may not be Jinn; they are

Angles.

CHAPTER SEVEN

ANGELS

Angels are creatures that God created from light, and therefore they literally have the speed of light. They are invisible and, just like Jinn, can take the form of anybody, but they don't take the form of animals, and in most cases, they take the form of handsome men. But this is not because they are males. Nobody knows if angels are males or not, but according to multiple verses in the Quran, they are definitely not females.

The Almighty Allah mentioned multiple times in the Quran that angels are not females. For example, in chapter 53 (Surah An-Najm), He said:

(Indeed, those who do not believe in the Hereafter name the angels with female names, though they have no knowledge of that. They only follow assumptions, yet surely assumptions do not substitute for the truth.)

Surah An-Najm, verses 27, 28

﴿ إِنَّ ٱلَّذِينَ لَا يُؤْمِنُونَ بِٱلْآخِرَةِ لَيُسَمُّونَ ٱلْمَلَئِكَةَ تَسْمِيَةَ ٱلْأُنثَىٰ * وَمَا لَهُم بِهِۦ مِنْ عِلْمٍ إِن يَتَّبِعُونَ إِلَّا ٱلظَّنَّ وَإِنَّ ٱلظَّنَّ لَا يُغْنِي مِنَ ٱلْحَقِّ شَيْئًا ﴾

So, If there are no females among them, they must have no sexual desires, which is what all Muslim scholars agree on.

They are not children, although they may play with children sometimes, and this reminds me of my 2-year-old nephew when he sometimes starts laughing for no reason and points to a corner of the room where there is nothing visible there. It's as if he can see something that I can't.

Angels also don't need to eat or drink, and this is evident in verses of the Quran that talk about when the angels visited the prophet Ibrahim. In Surah Athareyaat, it says:

(Has the story of Abraham's [Ibrahim] honored guests reached you? When they entered upon him, they said, "Peace." He said, "Peace, strangers." And he slipped away to his family and brought a fatted calf and set it before them. He said, "Will you not eat?" And he was filled with apprehension towards them. They said, "Do not be afraid," and they announced to him the glad tidings of a knowledgeable boy.)

Surah Athareyaat, verses 24-28

﴿ هَلْ أَتَىٰكَ حَدِيثُ ضَيْفِ إِبْرَٰهِيمَ ٱلْمُكْرَمِينَ * إِذْ دَخَلُواْ عَلَيْهِ فَقَالُواْ سَلَـٰمًا قَالَ سَلَـٰمٌ قَوْمٌ مُّنكَرُونَ * فَرَاغَ إِلَىٰ أَهْلِهِۦ فَجَآءَ بِعِجْلٍ سَمِينٍ * فَقَرَّبَهُۥٓ إِلَيْهِمْ قَالَ أَلَا تَأْكُلُونَ * فَأَوْجَسَ مِنْهُمْ خِيفَةً قَالُواْ لَا تَخَفْ وَبَشَّرُوهُ بِغُلَـٰمٍ عَلِيمٍ ﴾

And it is from Allah's wisdom that He made angels don't have desires like humankind because they are so numerous and incredibly huge, and if you wonder how huge they are, just imagine that one angel can crush two mountains together. So, they are not just huge but also have a tremendous force.

***

When prophet Muhammed, peace be upon him, saw Angle Jibreel for the first time, he saw the Angle in his real form. And he didn't know who he was. So, the Prophet went to his wife, shaking from fear, and said:
- "Cover me up, cover me up."

After that, The Prophet, peace be upon him, described Angel Jibreel when he saw him for the second time. He said that Angel Jibreel's wings blocked the whole sky, and he had 600 wings.
And speaking of wings, it's true that angels have wings, and the Almighty Allah told us in Surah Fater in the Holy Quran verse 1:

(All praise be to Allah, Originator of the heavens and the earth, Maker of the angels

as

messengers with two and three and four wings. He adds to creation as He wills; indeed, Allah is Powerful over everything.)

﴿ ٱلْحَمْدُ لِلَّهِ فَاطِرِ ٱلسَّمَـٰوَٰتِ وَٱلْأَرْضِ جَاعِلِ ٱلْمَلَـٰئِكَةِ رُسُلًا أُو۟لِىٓ أَجْنِحَةٍ مَّثْنَىٰ وَثُلَـٰثَ وَرُبَـٰعَ يَزِيدُ فِى ٱلْخَلْقِ مَا يَشَآءُ إِنَّ ٱللَّهَ عَلَىٰ كُلِّ شَىْءٍ قَدِيرٌ ﴾

The Almighty Allah mentioned in this verse that angels can have two, three, or four wings, and they can have more than that. Prophet Muhammad, peace be upon him, said:

- "I was allowed to speak about an angel from the angels of Allah who carry the Throne: (the distance) between his earlobe and shoulder covers a seven-hundred-years journey."

That distance, which you can cover, running for 700 years, is only the distance between his earlobe and his shoulder. So, imagine how huge He is.

Angels are intelligent creatures like jinn and humankind, except they are not accountable for their actions because they do whatever the

Almighty Allah commands them to do. They are not capable of disobeying the Almighty Allah, unlike humankind and Jinn.

They can also speak your language, and you can understand them if you contact them for any reason.

You may wonder why they don't contact us. Simply, our relationship with angels is regulated by the Almighty Allah.

If God orders them to do something, they will do it without hesitation, as Allah told us in the Quran in chapter 66, verse 6:

﴿ مَلَٰٓئِكَةٌ غِلَاظٌ شِدَادٌ لَّا يَعْصُونَ ٱللَّهَ مَآ أَمَرَهُمْ وَيَفْعَلُونَ مَا يُؤْمَرُونَ ﴾

(Fierce and powerful angels who never disobey Allah in anything He commands them, and they carry out whatever they are commanded)

Surah Attahreem.

So, How does the Almighty Allah regulate our relationship with angels, and what commands has He given them to carry out?

First: The Almighty Allah has informed us that each human being has two angels assigned to him from birth, whose only job is to record every word and deed in detail of their assigned person.

This is mentioned in Surah Qaaf of the Holy Quran, where Allah says:

(And surely, We created man and know what his (inner) self-whispers to him, for We are nearer to him than his jugular vein. As the two receptors [angels] receive (him), one on the right and one on the left, constantly seated. Not a word does he utter, but close to him is a watcher, constantly ready)

﴿ وَلَقَدْ خَلَقْنَا ٱلْإِنسَـٰنَ وَنَعْلَمُ مَا تُوَسْوِسُ بِهِۦ نَفْسُهُۥ وَنَحْنُ أَقْرَبُ إِلَيْهِ مِنْ حَبْلِ ٱلْوَرِيدِ * إِذْ يَتَلَقَّى ٱلْمُتَلَقِّيَانِ عَنِ ٱلْيَمِينِ وَعَنِ ٱلشَّمَالِ قَعِيدٌ * مَّا يَلْفِظُ مِن قَوْلٍ إِلَّا لَدَيْهِ رَقِيبٌ عَتِيدٌ ﴾

And in chapter 82, Surah - Al-Infitaar, the Almighty Allah says:

*(while indeed, over you are preservers—
honorable scribes— who know whatever you
do.)*

﴿ وَإِنَّ عَلَيْكُمْ لَحَـٰفِظِينَ * كِرَامًا كَـٰتِبِينَ * يَعْلَمُونَ مَا تَفْعَلُونَ ﴾

Surah - Al-Infitaar

So, there is no need to write your diary, my friend. Because your two angels are already doing that for you. In the Hereafter, you will receive the record of your deeds from them, and you will feel either pride or shame based on what they have done.

So, considering that every person has two angels assigned to them, that's in addition to the countless other angels fulfilling various tasks in both the earthly and heavenly realms. It's mind-boggling to think of just how many angels there must be.

***

The Almighty Allah has mentioned several angels in the Holy Quran by name and their duties.

For instance, Angel Jibreel was repeatedly mentioned by name or referred to as "the Spirit.". His primary responsibility was to deliver divine revelations from Allah to the prophets and messengers.

After delivering the last message of Islam, which is the Holy Quran to Prophet Muhammad (PBUH), he now visits the first heaven only once every year on the last ten days of Ramadan.

Another angel mentioned in the Quran is Angel Michael, who is responsible for the winds. He moves them wherever Allah commands him to move them and moves the clouds to cause rain to fall in certain countries according to Allah's command.

There is also Angel Israfeel; he holds the great trumpet and is waiting for Allah's command to blow it, which will signal the start of the end of the world.

There are also the angels of death who are responsible for taking the souls of all creatures when it is their time to depart, with the permission of the Almighty Allah.

And some angels continually worship Allah without getting tired and say:
"All Glory is to you, Allah. We are not worshipping you as we should."

Also, some angels guard and protect believers and children while they are sleeping or awake, and there are several stories about this.

My mother once shared a story with me from my nursery days about one of my classmates who fell from the fourth floor. You'd think he died from such a fall, but surprisingly, he actually only broke his leg. While he was in the hospital, he told his mom:
- Mom, I saw my uncle catching me.
But here's the thing, his uncle wasn't even there!

***

My brother-in-law told us about his mom. She said she saw a demon in her dream trying to kill her. Then, suddenly, a vast creature punched the demon in the face and told her:
- "Don't ever sleep alone again."
But at that time, her husband was traveling, so she was alone in the house with her son. She had the same dream again and saw the demon trying to squeeze her throat. Then, the huge creature came again, punched the demon, and told her:
- "I told you not to sleep alone again."

***

We all heard about the earthquake that hit Syria and Turkey. The children who stayed trapped under the rubble for days were asked how they survived without food or drink. They said: - There was an uncle who visited me every day and fed me. Another story that came out of this earthquake was when rescuers were about to remove the remains of a destroyed house using bulldozers. A woman appeared and told them that her children were still under the house's rubble. The rescuers pulled the debris by hand and found the children, but when they turned around, the woman was nowhere to be found, and when they asked the children about their mother, they responded that she had passed away two years ago.

You may be wondering why the angels didn't rescue the children from the rubble themselves and why they waited for the rescuers to do it.

This brings us to the first rule: our relationship with the angels is regulated by the Almighty Allah, and He is the one who decides when our time is up and when it isn't, and we are all going to die eventually; the only question is when.

Therefore, the angels themselves don't know when a person's time is up, except when Allah tells them, and as a result, they simply follow His commands and don't act on their own will.

***

So, after knowing all of this, it's natural to wish that they were always close to us. But how can we make sure that they are?

So, the first rule is to be clean.

Prophet Muhammad (peace be upon him) taught us that things that bother us as human beings bother the angels too. This includes bad smells from anywhere or anyone, bad breath, or unpleasant sounds during eating or burping. Also, try only to pass gas in the toilet as angels do not enter there; they wait for you outside.

In addition, angels do not enter places that are dirty or where dogs are present because, basically, dogs are not considered clean, especially their saliva, and in Islam, it is forbidden to raise dogs except for hunting or guarding purposes, and even then, the dog should be kept outside of the house or in a small place in the garden.

Also, wherever the Holy Quran is recited, the angels come to listen, and the presence of angels drives away the demons.

However, it is essential to remember that angels do not protect us without the permission of the Almighty Allah. So we must have faith that Allah is the One who protects us from anything that can harm us, whether it is visible or invisible creatures or even invisible things like

Envy.

CHAPTER EIGHT

ENVY

Until now, we have discussed paranormal creatures that can harm or benefit you with the permission of the Almighty Allah. But what about humans harming or even killing other humans without even touching them? This is where envy comes into play, and the Prophet Muhammad (peace be upon him) warned us about the envious eye and that it can sometimes even lead to death. Therefore, he advised us to constantly seek refuge in the Almighty Allah from the envious eye.

Envy, in simple terms, is when someone sees the blessings in your life and wishes for those blessings to be taken away from you and given to them instead.

Although the envious person's

wishes may be granted, it doesn't mean that the gift will be transferred to them.

The prophet Muhammad peace be upon him said:

- (If it were something that preceded fate, the eye would have preceded it).

This statement explains how the envious eye can quickly harm people, but it doesn't change your destiny. It may only be the means by which you reach your destiny.

Envy can affect anyone, even unintentionally, including those who love you.

Sometimes, you may even envy yourself or your belongings accidentally.

I once heard a man say that whenever he sees someone with something he wants, he feels a hot ray coming out of his eyes.

This makes me wonder about people who share their personal lives on social media or publicly post their income reports.

You may think I am exaggerating the idea of envy, so let me tell you a couple of stories that will make you understand how the envious eye can affect people:

A young man was reciting a poem in public and was doing a great job when suddenly he fell and was unable to move.

His mother later said in a voice recording:

- Please pray for my son to heal from his illness. He was completely fine, but when he recited his poem, he told me, "I looked at the crowd that was there and found a guy staring at me while I was reciting my poem, and I looked back to the phone to complete the poem but couldn't see anything. Then, I felt like I couldn't move my body, and I fell"

Now, he is in the hospital and unable to move his arm that was holding the phone.

***

I witnessed another story where a young lady posted a photo of her 2-year-old daughter on social media and jokingly said:

- (Who wants to take her?)

All the comments posted were saying:

- (Me, let me take her, I can't believe how beautiful she is).
And just half an hour later, a door fell on the little girl, and she died.

I came across a video on YouTube that captured a Lamborghini parked at a gas station. A random guy approached the car and just looked at it for a while, and suddenly, the car caught fire without any apparent cause.

Another guy shared his story on YouTube, where he posted a video on Snapchat and received a comment saying:
- Would you give me your hair?
The guy showed his head and beard on the camera, and his hair fell out, leaving him with big alopecia on his head and beard.
There are countless stories about the envious eye, and YouTube is full of videos showing moments caught on camera when people show their admiration about something, and suddenly an accident happens to that thing. These stories are more common in Arabic

content, and I can share some links that will leave no doubt that the envious eye is real:

https://www.youtube.com/watch?v=ZLqCMPH4E-I

https://www.youtube.com/watch?v=ymY2G57RswQ

https://www.youtube.com/watch?v=VgXjbStPMQ0

https://www.youtube.com/watch?v=U-gXFzpCz_4

https://www.youtube.com/watch?v=Sx5n6HWRGNQ

***

The Quran mentions the envious eye several times, and the Prophet Muhammad (peace be upon him) sought refuge for his grandsons from it. Interestingly, you can even unknowingly envy yourself just by admiring your own belongings without praying for blessings.

Envy doesn't always come from having something unique that others want. Some people just can't see anything good in what other people have.

A scholar once shared a story from the Middle Centuries about a man who told his visitors that he planned to move out of his neighborhood because his neighbors envied him.

The visitors were surprised because the man had nothing except a ball, a small bed, and some other essential items; the man was literally poor!

- The visitors asked: "How on earth do your neighbors envy you when you have nothing?".

- He said: "Wait, I'll show you." He raised his voice and said:

- "The king has summoned me to be executed alongside so-and-so,"

and he named three famous people.

His neighbors, who were listening from their window, exclaimed:

- "You will be executed with those famous people!".
It was clear that they couldn't even imagine him having a noble death!

***

The scholar told another story from the Middle Centuries about two people who were invited to the king's palace because they were famous for their envious eyes.
- The king said: "One of you make a request, and I'll give the other one the double of what I give to the first one.

The two men started to argue, neither wanted to ask first and missing out on the double reward until the king intervened and chose one of them to start.

- The man looked at the king and said: "Okay king, take one of my eyes."
And this is just because he couldn't even imagine the other man getting the double reward.

***

Prophet Muhammad (peace be upon him) was told about one of his companions (Sahl) who was very ill. So, when the prophet saw Sahl's poor condition, he asked the people who caused it; the crowd said:

- "Amer ibn Rabia looked at him with admiration."

(when he saw Sahl's white skin.)

The prophet (PBUH) said:

- "Why would one of you kill his brother? If you see something beautiful, wouldn't you say, 'God bless it'?"

So, the prophet (PBUH) then told Amer ibn Rabia to wash his face, his arms to the elbow, and his legs to the knees, and the prophet used that water to wash Sahl's body.

So, Sahl woke up actively and was healed as if he had never been ill.

From that story, we learned from the prophet (PBUH) that if we doubt that a particular person envied us, we should take the water that he washes his face with or anything from his clothes and mix it with some water and use it to wash our bodies. And when we see something admirable, we should wish and pray that God blesses that thing or that person and always seek refuge by the Almighty Allah from envious eyes.

One soldier from Saudi Arabia posted a video of himself showing the badges that he received while serving in the army because one of his followers asked him about his experience in the military, but later, he appeared on a TV show and he was crippled, he revealed that he had become completely paralyzed after posting that video, He said:

- "One of my friends posted to my followers, asking them to pray for me to be cured of the illness, and a follower visited me in the hospital and told me that the envious eye is real, and maybe he envied me without meaning to do so. So he washed my body with the water that he washed his face with, and as soon as he did that, I was able to sit upright; although I'm still crippled and can't move the lower part of my body, at least I became able to move the upper part now."

***

Some people may believe that those with envious eyes have the power to destroy lives as if it's some sort of gift. However, the reality is that the jealous person faces punishment for his envy even before his actions take effect. Just imagine that no one wants to be around him, and it reminds me of one of my sister's friends. My sister told me that whenever her friend group has an occasion, nobody invites this girl because of her envious eye. Every time she sees or talks to that girl, she's always deeply depressed. It's like all success, and good luck have been taken from her life. It's as if she doesn't like to see anybody better than her or any gift in other people's hands, but as a result, she never sees any goodness in her life too.

***

In the Middle East, you can find items that people believe can protect them from the envious eye, like the blue bead or the Hamsa, which is a hand-shaped amulet, or other types of trinkets that people wear on necklaces:

But they are all nonsense and have proved their failure in protecting anybody from envy. The only thing that can genuinely save you is seeking refuge in the Almighty Allah. He has all the power and knowledge of your situation, and sometimes He sends messages to warn you, like

visions.

CHAPTER NINE

VISIONS

The Prophet Muhammad (peace be upon him) once said:

- (There is nothing left after me from the prophecy except the missionaries,

- they said: O Messenger of Allah, what are the missionaries?

- He said: The good vision, the man sees it, or it is seen for him).

In another speech, the Prophet (peace be upon him) stated that a good vision is one of the 46 parts of prophecy. Of course, this doesn't mean that having a good vision equates to having a prophecy, but it does signify that the Almighty Allah has sent a message or warning to the person.

***

The prophets are protected from the influence of the devils, so their visions are more accurate and clearer, like the moon shining in the dark, but for regular people, the devil may try to manipulate their dreams.

For instance, one of the companions asked the Prophet, peace be upon him, about a dream he had that he saw his head rolling on the ground and he was running after it.
The Prophet, peace be upon him, replied that it was just Satan trying to manipulate him.

So, the closer you are to Allah by remembering Him and worshipping Him, the more protected you will be from the devils, and your dream visions will be moretransparent and easier to understand. The Quran also talks a lot about visions, like in Surah Yusuf (Joseph) in chapter 12, where Allah describes Prophet Yusuf as talented in explaining visions.

The chapter starts with the story that Prophet Yusuf, peace be upon him, told his father, Prophet Yaqoob (Jacob):

- (O father, I saw the sun, the moon, and 11 planets prostrating for me).

His father responded:

- (O son, don't tell your brothers about your dream because they might get jealous and plot against you because of envy, Satan is a clear enemy to the man).

It's clear from Prophet Yaqoob's advice that if you see something good in your dream, don't tell anybody except those who genuinely love and care for you, and it's better not to talk about it at all.

In that chapter, you will learn about the story of Prophet Yusuf, including what happened to him until his dream became true, and his parents and his 11 brothers prostrated before him.

So, a vision might refer to the future or the present that you can never know about it except by a message from the Almighty Allah.

I came across a story about a murder case where investigators couldn't find the victim's body. The victim's mother tried to convince the investigators to search the lake, but they told her:

- "If your son is in the lake, the crocodiles would eat him."

After the mother insisted, they finally found the body and caught the murderers. The mother said she saw her son regularly in her dreams, asking her to take him out of the lake. And when you see a dead person in your dream telling you something, then whatever they say is 99% true because they are in the transparent place, the hereafter. However, it's possible for the devil to take the form of a dead person to manipulate you.

But there is one dead person whom the devil cannot take his form, and that's the prophet Muhammad peace be upon him. Because He said:

- (Whoever sees me in their dreams, they see me because the devil cannot take my form.).

So, if you hear the prophet Muhammad, peace be upon him, say something in your dream, be sure it's a fact.

***

This is for the good vision, but when it comes to bad dreams, the Prophet Muhammad, peace be upon him, advised that if you have an uncomfortable dream, spit on your left side three times and seek refuge in the Almighty Allah from the accursed devil, and don't tell anyone about it.

However, not all dreams that make you uncomfortable are from the devil, a sometimes Allah may send you some warnings.

For instance, once I opened my eyes and I saw a huge anaconda in my room staring at me.
I closed my eyes again, trying to play dead, but then I realized it might be a devil. So, I started reciting the last two chapters of the Quran, and the anaconda turned into a woman and ran

away. Then I woke up and realized that a woman is trying to hurt me by sorcery.

In Surah A-Shurah, Chapter 42 of the Quran, verse 51, Allah says:

(And it is not for any human that Allah should speak to him except by revelation or from behind a veil or by sending a messenger to reveal by His permission whatever He wills; indeed, He is All-High, All-Wise.)

﴿ ۞ وَمَا كَانَ لِبَشَرٍ أَن يُكَلِّمَهُ ٱللَّهُ إِلَّا وَحْيًا أَوْ مِن وَرَآيِ حِجَابٍ أَوْ يُرْسِلَ رَسُولًا فَيُوحِيَ بِإِذْنِهِۦ مَا يَشَآءُ إِنَّهُۥ عَلِيٌّ حَكِيمٌ ﴾

Therefore, if you receive a message from Allah, it will be through messengers who left the divine revelation in the Holy Book [The Quran] or through true visions in your dreams. And an exceptional vision will have exceptional features, such as being straightforward to understand. No matter how much time goes by, it's unforgettable and easy to narrate, just like movies.

For instance, my mother had a vision after her father passed away, in which he took her one- year-old son with him. She shared this vision with us only after my elder brother died at the age of 23, which was 22 years later after she saw that vision.

Of course, keeping the vision a secret didn't change the destiny or delay it, as the time of death for every person is predetermined and cannot be delayed or hastened.

But if that uncomfortable dream wasn't about death, you can avoid anything that could harm you in the future by asking Almighty Allah for protection and seeking His mercy and guidance.

The Prophet Muhammad (peace be upon him) said that destiny and supplication tussle between heaven and earth till the day of resurrection.

And if God [Almighty Allah] is the One Who Creates destiny, then He is the One Who Changes it, and this is clear in the Holy Quran, in chapter 13:

(Allah Erases whatever He Decides and He Keeps (whatever He Decides), and with Him is the source of the Scripture.)

﴿ يَمْحُوا۟ ٱللَّهُ مَا يَشَآءُ وَيُثْبِتُ وَعِندَهُۥٓ أُمُّ ٱلْكِتَـٰبِ ﴾

Surah a-Rra'd, verse 39

***

When it comes to interpreting visions, there are often clear signs that can help you understand the message being conveyed.

For instance, if you see scorpions or gorillas in your vision, it may indicate that someone has envied you.

On the other hand, if you see snakes, magicians, or gorillas, it may indicate that someone is attempting to harm you through sorcery - and snakes are the most common symbol for this.

If you see cats or wild dogs, it could mean you have an enemy from the Jinn.

If you see a cockroach, it could indicate a sin that you have to repent for.

Seeing beautiful toddlers might signify a bright future, mainly if they were girls.

Spiders or crows may indicate abandoned places where the Quran is not recited, and if you see crows on someone's head, it could mean that their time to depart from this life is approaching.

Seeing money or gold in your vision could be a sign that whoever took it in your dream will become wealthy.

Seeing delicious food may be a sign of a blessing you will receive from Allah.

Generally speaking, if you see something clean, beautiful, or delicious, it's likely a good omen, whereas if you see something dirty, ugly, or scary, it may represent something negative.

And I say [it may] because nobody can be sure about the exact meaning of a dream, and we rely on the signs mentioned in the Quran to interpret them. But moreover, we may not understand the precise meaning of a vision because simply, we are not prophets. Moreover, reciting the Ruqia daily and reading Chapter 2 of the Quran as much as possible can protect you against harm.

Ultimately, we should seek Allah's protection and trust in His guidance.

If you receive a missionary in your dream, accept it as it is [a missionary] and don't overthink about it; just be happy, keep it a secret, and strive to make your life the best it can be.

***

In the end, I only included the information that is necessary for people to know about it, just to understand how to deal with this unseen world. So, don't try to search for more information because the consequences won't please you at all.

You might find it difficult to believe everything written in this book. I understand that if you've been living in a small room, everything outside of it may seem supernatural.

However, if you were once just a tiny drop of blood in your mother's womb, and then you grew into a full person in just nine months and considered that a natural process, so all the creatures that God Has Created are natural too, it's just you have never known about them before because they are beyond a veil that the Almighty Allah Created to Allow us to live our lives without being terrified all the time and to Test us: who will believe and who will disbelieve.
And don't worry, that veil will be removed one day when you see the angle of death when it's time for your soul to leave your body.

(Indeed, you were oblivious to this, so We removed your veil, and your sight today is (as sharp as) iron.)

﴿ لَّقَدْ كُنتَ فِي غَفْلَةٍ مِّنْ هَـٰذَا فَكَشَفْنَا عَنكَ غِطَآءَكَ فَبَصَرُكَ ٱلْيَوْمَ حَدِيدٌ ﴾

Surah-Qaaf, verse 22

AN HONEST REVIEW

You can help more readers to know the benefits they can get from reading the book by leaving your honest review and your **experience with the book.**

You can use any of the following links or Qr codes to leave a review: -

https://www.scribd.com/book/644628513/Beyond-the-Veil .

https://www.thalia.de/shop/home/artikeldetails/A106 8748255 .

https://www.smashwords.com/books/view/1392493?ref= .

https://www.angusrobertson.com.au/ebooks/beyond-the-veil-tasbeeh-ahmad/p/9798223312574 .

https://books.mondadoristore.it/Beyond-the-Veil-Tasbeeh-Ahmad/eae979822331257/ .

https://shop.vivlio.com/product/9798223312574_9798 223312574_T0020/beyond-the-veil .

https://market.thepalaceproject.org/item/5491059 .

https://books.apple.com/nl/book/beyond-the-veil/id6449040947 .

https://www.barnesandnoble.com/w/beyond-the-veil-tasbeeh-ahmad/1143474570;jsessionid=1F029664B6B95DDD75 DD96493687F26E.prodny_store02-atgap06?ean=2940167570016 .

SUBSCRIBE FOR

NEWSLETTER

Get access to exclusive stories and information that I don't share in my books.
Be the first one who gets access to free chapters of the upcoming new book releases.
I love to surprise my readers with fun little gifts. In my newsletters, you'll find special offers and free goodies.

Subscribe now

https://preview.mailerlite.io/preview/46
2763/forms/9363172214440400522

ABOUT THE AUTHOR

I'm an Egyptian Quran teacher who teaches Quran and basic Arabic to English speakers; I see the study of religion and science as complementary rather than separate. As an Egyptian Quran teacher, I aim to share my knowledge and understanding of the Quran and Arabic language with English speakers. I believe that the only way to seek knowledge about whatever is beyond the human's vision or expertise is to seek it from the creator of the entire realm, God.